The Snaggetty-Boggitt

By

Christopher Bramley

Copyright © 2016 Christopher Bramley

http://www.christopherbramley.co.uk

Art by Hannah Hopgood

Contact her at hannahkhopgood@yahoo.com

All rights reserved.

ISBN-13: 978-0-9931273-9-7

Once there were two little girls. They were sisters, and loved to play.

   The oldest was sometimes called Spoh, and she was fair haired and blue-eyed, like a bright sunflower and the blue sky above.

   The youngest was sometimes called Evester, and she was brown haired and blue eyed, like deep rich earth and the blue sea.

One morning they went into the back garden to play and saw the gate was open.

Spoh remembered mummy and daddy had said never go outside alone. But she could not see them and it looked interesting outside. It felt naughty to go out when they were told they could not, but it was fun, so they looked outside.

'Ooh, dear,' sang a little voice behind them. It sounded a bit like a mouse and a bit like a frog.

Spoh and Evester looked around. There was no one there. But there was a piles of leaves and some plants.

The voice spoke again. 'You mustn't go out there.'

'Why?' they said.

'Because it is dangerous on your own. You must never go without your parents.'

They looked in the leaves. A little lumpy green creature with black beady eyes and a wide mouth moved away quickly. It had a pointy nose and big cheeks with spindly legs and arms.

'Are you a monster?' said Spoh.

'A MONSTER!' cried the voice from somewhere else in the bush. There was a loud *BURP!* The little black eyes twinkled out.

'I'm just a poor old snaggetty-boggitt.'

'Snaggitt!' said Evester.

BURP!

'I'm not a *snagitt*. I am not a *Boggit* or a *Baggart* or a *Bogbear* or a *Buzzard* or a *Binglemingle*. I am a SNAGGETTY-BOGGITT. It means I am a boggitt that is snaggetty in every way. If you are nasty I shall go away.'

'Oh, don't go away, you old Snaggetty-Boggitt!' Spoh sang.

'Well, you must be nice to me then.'

'What's snaggetty?'

'It's what a boggitt is.'

'What are you doing?' said Spoh.

'I am being snaggetty. That means I live in hidden places under leaves. We watch people but only children can see us.

Any time you see small bushes move and hear the leaves rustle with a little burp-' the voice said *BURP!* '-you know a snaggetty-boggitt is near.'

Evester laughed. 'Burping!'

'It's our excited noise,' said the Snaggetty-Boggitt in a huffy way.

'I never heard you before,' said Spoh.

'Sometimes we say hello to children. It is nice to see you play. We wish we could too, all day. But we can't. We hide under plants and leaves in the nice dirt. We love the green glow of the sun, the pitter patter of the rain, the *crick crack!* of the frost.'

'Play with us,' said Evester.

'We can't come out from under the leaves for long. We turn into mist, *poof*, and have to wait until night again. But any time children are naughty or in trouble, be sure a snaggetty-boggitt is watching. That's why I said you mustn't go out of the gate.'

'Why not?' said Spoh. It looked exciting out there.

'*Because,*' burped the snaggetty-boggitt excitedly. 'It is dangerous! Look!'

Spoh and Evester looked at the gate. It looked nice outside. Suddenly a very fast car went past and made them jump.

WHOOSH!

'See?' The Snaggetty-Boggitt burped loudly, then sang:

*'Always do what you are told
So that you can grow up old
That car's fast, imagine that
If it hit you, you'd go splat!'*

The bush shook as he danced. 'It is dangerous without mummy or daddy. I'm just a poor old Snaggetty-Boggitt and I can't help you if you go SPLAT.'

Just then mummy called from the house. 'Lunch is ready!'

Spoh and Evester said, 'Will we see you again?'

Little black eyes in a lumpy green face watched them.

'Be good girls and do
what your parents say
And you will see me
On another day!'

Bye-Bye you old snaggetty-
boggitt!

ABOUT THE AUTHOR

Chris usually writes adult Fantasy, but he also has nieces, and a mental age that suits.

Find more of his work at his website, www.christopherbramley.co.uk

www.ingramcontent.com/pod-product-compliance
Lightning Source LLC
Chambersburg PA
CBHW041230040426
42444CB00002B/115